LAVISH FLOWERS

LAVISH FLOWERS

PEACH PANFILI

Photographs by RAY JOYCE

Angus&Robertson
An imprint of HarperCollins*Publishers*

Angus&Robertson

An imprint of HarperCollins*Publishers,* Australia

First published in Australia in 1994
This paperback edition published in 1996
by HarperCollins*Publishers* Pty Limited
ACN 009 913 517
A member of the HarperCollins*Publishers* (Australia) Pty Limited Group

Copyright © Diana Panfili and Ray Joyce 1994, 1996

HarperCollins*Publishers*
25 Ryde Road, Pymble, Sydney, NSW 2073, Australia
31 View Road, Glenfield, Auckland 10, New Zealand
Hazelton Lanes, 55 Avenue Road, Suite 2900, Toronto, Ontario M5R 3L2
and 1995 Markham Road, Scarborough, Ontario M1B 5M8, Canada
10 East 53rd Street, New York NY 10032, USA

National Library of Australia
Cataloguing-in-Publication data:
Panfili, Peach.
Lavish flowers.
ISBN 0 207 18998 6.
1. Flower arrangement. I. Title.
745.92

Printed in Hong Kong

9 8 7 6 5 4 3 2 1   96 97 98 99

In memory of Bebbie,

who always said

'Books are your best friends'.

ACKNOWLEDGMENTS

The inspiration for the arrangements in this book came from the flowers themselves, so it is the growers and purveyors of these beautiful blooms whom I must first acknowledge. Without their perseverance against the forces of nature (which, with a single brief hailstorm, can wipe out an entire season's work), their patience (be it bunching fifty tiny violets or propagating giant blooms from almost microscopic seed), or their dedication in searching out and procuring the very best from around the country and around the world, this book would not have been possible.

I would also like to acknowledge Michelle Wiener, who, after all-day sessions and late night phone calls, once our respective children were fed and bedded down, intuitively knew how I envisaged this book would look and brought the design to fruition. And Vanessa Rickard and Anna Holt for their creative input, and good humour, particularly in the running of 'Peach and Lavish', and Michaela Collins, who valiantly kept the numerical wheels turning and can now spot a less-than-fresh flower at fifty paces. Thanks are also due to the custodians of historic Vaucluse House, and to Robert and Sally Molines and Michael and Suzie O'Connor of the Peppertree Estate, for allowing us to use their beautiful properties as locations for some of the shots. And to John Olsen for his permission to reproduce his painting 'Squid In Its Own Ink' on page 82.

A special thank you goes to Jimmy and Toula Koustouvardes, who supply me with fresh fruit and vegetables, flowers and friendship. And to my loyal little friends, Lucia and Dominic, who tiptoed gingerly around expensive photographic equipment, proudly presented me with beautiful posies (the contents of which often came from neighbouring gardens), enthusiastically neglected their homework, and even, eventually, learnt to make their own toast, whilst their mother was 'busy doing her book'.

Finally, and most importantly, my gratitude goes to Ray Joyce, for his gentle patience and artist's eye.

TABLE OF CONTENTS

INTRODUCTION

'If a man has two pieces of bread,
he should give one to the poor, and sell the other
to buy a hyacinth to feed his soul.'
TRADITIONAL SAYING

Arranging flowers is really not so hard! People are too often intimidated by what they wrongly perceive as the intricate skills required to produce the type of arrangement which is wrapped, bedecked with ribbons and delivered to the door by a florist.

Rather than being a 'how to' book on flower arranging, full of Latin botanical names, *Lavish Flowers* has been designed to provide encouragement, information and inspiration to all those with a passion for flowers. Certainly a strong interest, desire or direction is a prerequisite for success. But all else is an easily learned skill. Just as boiling an egg takes time to master, so does flower arranging.

To 'play' with flowers is an absolute joy. In fact, play it must be and a joy it will be! However, as with cooking, the best ingredients are essential.

A fresh and perfect tulip or rose, standing alone in a vase, will give far greater pleasure in the long run than a hastily thrown-together mixed bunch, bought by the side of the road. Whereas the mixed bunch will, more often than not, stand stiff for a day then sadly wither and die, the tulip will turn towards the light, open, bend, become transparent, then drop her pollen and lastly her petals. Similarly, the rose will slowly bloom, bend back her calyx, grow fat in the vase, then finally and gracefully fade.

With this single perfect bloom you will have witnessed a season, rather than a death.

1

BRIGHT

The majority of flowers asked for by customers are by far bright and happy coloured arrangements, for very obvious reasons — bright colours signify happiness and cheer. There is a very simple colour formula which seems to work easily if shapes and sizes of flowers are also taken into account. For instance, a jug of yellow, orange, hot pink, purple and blue flowers incorporates both the warm and cool ends of the colour spectrum. The combination of these colours is what makes them sing, and adding white or a pastel will provide a highlight, although sometimes these paler tones will take away from the vibrancy of the brights and break up the overall effect. If you are unsure, a good benchmark to use is that if the shades of flowers you choose live happily side by side in the garden, they will most probably exist aesthetically together indoors.

The placing of flowers in a room is extremely important — why, I ask, stick a beautiful vase of gorgeous fresh flowers on a table by a window which is passed by only occasionally? Instead, put your flowers by the phone or by your bed, or by the bathroom sink so you can look at them and smell them as

Yellow tiger lilies, alstromeria, wild yellow cosmos and everlasting daisies are combined in a tight posy (above). The cosmos, which also comes in whites, pinks and purple shades, is as easily grown in the garden as by the side of the road. If the flowers are left to self-seed, they will return every year in even greater profusion.

A mass of mixed yellow flowers in a blue and white Chinese bowl (right) is enlivened by the addition of purple and burgundy freesias, nasturtiums picked by the side of the road, and the fluffy and almost fluorescent heads of bright purple liatris.

A Mexican tin tub is used as a container for iris, gerberas, sunflowers, Irish bells and oriental lilies. The Irish bells will last for weeks and are deliciously and unexpectedly perfumed. They will, however, curl towards the light. They will also dry successfully although they will not hold their colour unless dried using silica gel.

you clean your teeth. If your budget is limited, forget the sitting room or the front entrance if you normally relax in the back room and your guests usually arrive at the back door.

Two or three bunches of a simple flower like daisies or calendulas may, when in season, be equal in cost to one bunch of travel-weary imported flowers and will often last longer. The secret here is the container. Do not restrict yourself to vases, as often vases are designed by people who know little about flowers. Let your imagination run riot. Place daisies in baskets, terracotta pots or milk jugs.

This lovely display sits against a wall opposite a kitchen window and consists of clipped box, bulbs, perennials and annuals. The cyclamens and tulips can be brought inside for short periods to brighten up a room which may not be often used. Potted plants are the best way to brighten up gardens with little space. Once the bulbs have finished flowering and the foliage has died down, they can either be left in the pot and moved to a less used and sheltered part of the garden, or pulled up and stored in brown paper bags or old stockings in a cool, dry place until next season, when they can be planted out again. For the best results the following year, however, a spell in the refrigerator before planting will trick the bulbs into thinking that winter has arrived. Then, when planted in the warmer environment, a tulip or a daffodil will assume that spring has arrived and proceed to grow and flower. Annuals such as primulas can be let go to seed and although the flowers may not be as vigorous as the seedlings bought from a nursery, they can be quite prolific.

Yellow ranunculus and blue statice. Statice is one of the easiest flowers to dry and will hold its colour extremely well. Simply strip any foliage from about halfway down and hang upside down in a dry, dark place. The flowers can then be used for dried arrangements or potpourri, or can even be mixed with fresh flowers.

Rummage through your kitchen cupboards for biscuit tins, the garden shed for forgotten containers or even the children's toy box: a child's brightly coloured sand bucket makes a wonderful container for calendulas.

It is not necessary to have a cupboard full of Lalique and sterling silver as the flowers you choose will dictate the shape and colour of the container.

It is not necessary to own a cupboard full of beautiful vases to make beautiful arrangements. Here, a plastic icecream container placed inside a square biscuit tin makes a bright and simple base for flowers for a family room. These include sunflowers, gerberas, tulips, irises, Irish bells, and pelargoniums picked from the garden.

This arrangement (left) is
the focal point in the foyer of a
small hotel. Because it is a
public area, the arrangement
needs to be large. With
blossoms and tortured willow in
place, a riot of pacific giant
delphinium, gladioli, stock and
gerberas is added, followed
by flowers with finer stems, like
liatris and antherium lilies.

A posy of blue (above) is
contrasted against a background
of yellow ribbon, giving a
clear indication as to why this
universally loved combination
of colours works so well. The
blue flowers include Dutch
iris, butterfly delphinium and
old-fashioned cottage garden
favourites such as cornflowers,
love-in-a-mist, and salvia.

These lovely, bright anemones (above) come in shades of deep blue-purple to cyclamen pink and rich red. Many will have a stark white ring around their velvety centres and are very easy to grow. Other varieties, known commonly as Japanese windflowers or wind anemones, grow much taller on delicate stems from luxuriant clumps of foliage which hug the ground, and come in more pastel shades of pink and white. The strength of this arrangement (right) lies in its simplicity. An old blue jug is filled with vibrant anemones, clover grass and weeds, and placed on the weathered wooden windowsill of an old kitchen, giving inspiration to those carrying out a dreary chore. Even a little jug of buttercups on a laundry shelf is a far more cheerful alternative to boxes of soap powder and bottles of bleach. Place your flowers where you will get the most enjoyment from them. If your sitting room is only used once a week you may be better off buying a flowering plant and moving the flowers next to the kitchen sink or beside the bed.

There are many different types of daffodils. The variety here (left) has a lovely double-ruffled trumpet. It has been combined simply with a big bunch of field carnations. Try to buy daffodils when they are still tightly closed and fresh. Daffodils are one of the few flowers where recutting the stem is not such a wise idea, as the slimy sap that bleeds from their stems is incompatible with some flowers such as tulips, and will in turn shorten the vase life of the tulip. However, as they both bloom in spring and live happily together in the garden, I often can't resist forcing the friendship and placing them together.

The lovely muted flowers of helleborus (above), often called winter rose, appear in profusion in cold climate gardens, and are wonderful mixed in posies or just simply used on their own.

These bright tropical
heliconia (above) are very long-
lived. Some varieties are
known as 'crab claws', for
obvious reasons. Others
which hang on dangling stems
from the end of stiff rods
are often called fishing poles or
hanging heliconia.
As the flowers do not develop
further once harvested,
it is important to buy them
fully developed. Here they have
been mixed with lilies and
palm seeds in an antique pitcher,
and set starkly against
a bright blue wall.
When choosing red roses (right)
be aware of the options
offered by different varieties.
Those with a stronger
perfume such as 'Mr Lincoln'
will blow quickly and won't last
as long in the vase as varieties
such as 'Samantha' which
exchange scent for lasting power .

The dahlia is such a lovely, happy flower (above). It was much prized by the Empress Josephine, although legend has it that she had all her dahlias dug up and destroyed after discovering the theft of one of her prized tubers. The number of varieties of these sunny flowers is astounding, ranging from the softest, palest pastels with rounded petals to the multi-coloured spiky types, which look more like sea anemones than flowers. Watch out for draughts and direct sunlight, as their succulent petals will not prove hardy enough to withstand the drying effects these conditions may cause. Lovely papery poppy blooms (right), so aptly named, will open if placed in the sunshine. When picking poppies, make sure you always pick them when the hairy buds are round and fat. Recut the stems and place them in 2.5 cm (1 in) of boiling water to seal the ends. However, be careful not to allow the heads to come in contact with the steam while doing this. If you buy poppies from a flower shop, this will have already been done for you. Occasionally you will find poppies for sale that have been picked when open. These will also last very well. The only thing to look out for in this situation is damage to the delicate petals — just be gentle and carry them home carefully.

This low table centrepiece (above) is made up of a base of glossy green angelica leaves, roses, sweet peas and white carnations, and has been arranged in a shallow tray containing florist foam, which allows the flowers to spill out onto the table.

Some of the oriental lilies in this arrangement (right) have had their stamens removed, while others have not. To avoid staining, the stamens must be removed before they become dark and powdery, and before the lilies open up like big white stars. Both the lilies and

the delicate white iris have fine, bending stems and are therefore suitable for a straight, narrow container. The tall metallic pitcher they share will provide them with little space, so a bending stem will allow them to lean beyond the confines of the vase, giving a softer, looser shape.

A tight posy of miniature daisies, roses, sweet peas and godetia is contrasted with black satin ribbons (above). The ribbons, which are separately looped and wired, not only serve a decorative purpose but also hold the flowers in shape. This type of posy is most suitable for hospitals where the air conditioning will lead to a quicker than usual deterioration of flowers. The backgrounds against which your arrangements are placed are very important. If these same flowers (right) were positioned against a yellow wall, the white petals of the daisies would visually jump out. Similarly, against a white wall, the petals would disappear and the yellow centres would become the focus.

Big branches of oak leaves and gold-sprayed twigs and holly form the base to which large spikes of double delphinium, roses and oriental lilies have been added. The container is a simple terracotta pot painted with blackboard paint, which dries quickly to give a very matt surface.

A single rose the colour
of clotted cream, if picked at this
stage, will give days of pleasure
and also force the rose bush to
produce again. Even if you choose
to keep your roses outside and
on the bush, you will be rewarded
with a bigger crop if the blooms
that have faded are cut back to a
shoot at an angle. This will
cause the bush to bloom
again rather than produce fruit
— that is, the rosehips, which
in many cases are far more
spectacular at the end of
the flowering season, when they
can be picked for their own
particular, glossy beauty.

*Clumps of daisies in simple
tin buckets line a pathway and
make a strong yet casual
and inexpensive statement in
an outdoor setting.*

Creamy November lilies share
the same strappy leaves
as many of the other lily
varieties. They also share
the habit of these leaves turning
yellow and unsightly long
before the flowers are spent.
Here, the lilies have been
contrasted against glossy green
camellia leaves — a most
hardy and long-lived foliage that
can be used over and over
again, outliving almost anything
it is teamed up with.

Many flowers, such as delphinium and snapdragons, do not have lush foliage. Here (left) a branch of frangipani foliage is used as filler, together with delphinium, snapdragon, and a few stems of garden roses for contrast. One of the few instances where 'torture' is acceptable in floristry is in the wiring of wedding flowers (above), be they in a formal teardrop- shaped bouquet, a sheath which is carried over the arm, a headdress for a flower girl or a deceptively simple posy. It must be remembered that the flowers used on these occasions will be out of water, handled, photographed, and pressed against during the congratulatory kisses and embraces after the ceremony, and fiddled with by shy little girls unused to circlets, hoops or posies, or the excitement of the day. Without wire, a florist would be unable to fashion a large, tight, full posy without the stem section becoming too large to be comfortable to carry in a dainty bridesmaidlike fashion, or so heavy that the bride totters rather than glides down the aisle.

The very large and handsome magnolia can grow to massive proportions and is therefore not suitable for a small garden. Its creamy white, almost suede-like blossoms (above) are highly perfumed. Originally from the Orient, the magnolia is also a species found in the Americas. It became popular as a shade tree and has always reminded me of the era depicted in 'Gone With the Wind'. The magnificent blooms are better left on the tree as, once picked, they retain their habit of closing up at night and may remain shut in the vase.

A combination of blowzy 'Mt Shasta' roses and dainty sprays of 'Iceberg' roses (right). Although 'Mt Shasta' open quickly to reveal their golden stamens, the petals, if left undisturbed, will hang on the stem for a week or more. The perennial favourite, 'Iceberg' is one of the few truly remontant, least temperamental and most rewarding roses, and with the cold weather will often develop a lovely mushroomy-pink tinge to its outside petals. Being a spray variety, as long as the spent flowers are removed, the new buds will continue to open.

3

INSPIRATION

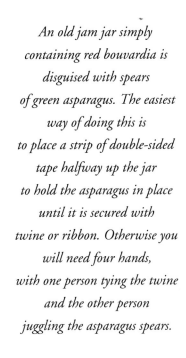

*An old jam jar simply
containing red bouvardia is
disguised with spears
of green asparagus. The easiest
way of doing this is
to place a strip of double-sided
tape halfway up the jar
to hold the asparagus in place
until it is secured with
twine or ribbon. Otherwise you
will need four hands,
with one person tying the twine
and the other person
juggling the asparagus spears.*

Calendulas and kale, sunflowers, bright purple liatris, green Irish bells and leaves of cut palm are contrasted against a teal-coloured wall (above). The palm has been used to emphasise the shape of the modern glass slab vase, with the colours of the flowers inspired by the painting hung beside them.

Sunflowers (right) can be tricky — if they are scalded when they are picked their vase life is long and rewarding. However, if too much time has elapsed before scalding takes place, they will hang their heavy seed-filled heads, and their petals and leaves will shrivel away. The sunflower is another example of

a flower which will more often than not outlive its foliage, and it is mostly better to strip it of its wilting leaves and place it in a vase with a more interesting companion. Here a flower associated with summer and heat is teamed up with branches of autumn-coloured maple leaves.

The simplicity of calla lilies has been emphasised by using these flowers only and arranging them in a clump that is similar in shape to that of a single lily.

Bare magnolia branches (left)
have been placed in the vase first
to help hold the heavy
aloe vera in place. The vase has
then been filled with gorgeous
oriental lilies in white and pink.
Although it is an expensive
combination, the lasting power
of this arrangement is almost
unchallenged.

The until recently much-
maligned carnation (above) is
now coming back into
fashion as a cut flower. Here a
stripy variegated variety is
teamed with green goddess lilies
and aloe vera. All these
flowers are very long-lasting,
with the carnations being easily
propagated from cuttings.

Globe artichokes with long stems and leaves intact have been mixed with gold-sprayed grasses to form a screen in a restaurant. Moss dyed a deep rust camouflages the base of the stems and provides a warm contrast between the pots and their contents.

This arrangement of muted coloured flowers (near right) includes the pointy Russell lupin, which comes in many gorgeous dusty shades. Russell lupins need to be treated in order to stop them dropping their pea-like flowers. There are also hydrangeas, as well as two types of lilies. The gloriosa or glory lily is in fact a vine which has tendrils that attach themselves to whatever happens to be closest to them in the vase.

Flowers in muted tones of dusty pink and burgundy, combined with the coffee-coloured 'Julia's Rose', sit in a square container (far right). Also included in this arrange-ment are alstromeria or Peruvian lilies, calla lilies and deep, rusty red dahlias.

A terracotta pot painted with matt blackboard paint (left) is used as a container to hold lush purple kale (ornamental cabbage) and liatris, together with large, bright green broccoli florets. The liatris echoes the rich colour of the cabbage. The kale will last well if its stem has been picked long enough for it to drink, whereas the broccoli will yellow with age, and will have to be replaced.

These dahlias, the colour of Spanish onions (above), are one of the many different varieties being developed today. The main thing to watch for when buying these lovely, luscious, flashy flowers is that their stems are strong and thick enough to carry their heavy heads. Always take care when handling dahlias as they are extremely delicate, with their petals being easily creased and bruised.

A table centrepiece is given
a different feel by combining
flowers and vegetables (near
right). Black-eyed gerberas and
blue brodiaea are placed in first,
followed by sweet peppers and
broccoli florets, which are
held in position using wooden
butchers' skewers.

Often the most effective
arrangements are the most
simple ones, and contain just
one type of flower. Here, a
granite container (far right)
has been used to emphasise the
strength and shape of this
clump of bright blue iris. A
length of cheap twine tied
halfway visually cuts the line of
green stems and also helps
the flowers to stand uniformly
to attention.

4

PASTEL

Traditionally it's assumed that the young, the elderly and the gentle are most often drawn to pretty, pastel flowers. If choice of colour is indicative of state of mind, then, while bright and cheerful flowers make us feel happy, soft pastel shades must surely reflect serenity and romance.

More often than not it is young girls who are drawn to delicate, pink, perfumed roses, although I've also spent many happy hours listening to poetic reminiscences about the lovely old fashioned Cécile Brünner roses which 'grew wild when I was a girl'.

Queen Anne's lace or cow
parsley (left) adds softness
to a basket of pastel stock, pink
ranunculus, snowdrops and
scabiosa or pincushion flowers.
The stems of lace are arranged
in a criss-cross pattern to
support the ranunculus, the stock
and, lastly, the smaller
snowdrops and scabiosa.
In this arrangement (right)
the soft, papery blooms and blue-
grey foliage of wild poppies
are used as a base, to which
Japanese ranunculus and
double pink tulips are added.
Although the poppies will
drop their petals quite quickly,
the young seed pods left
behind on the ends of furry,
spindly stems will outlive
the other flowers in the vase.

A generous jug of fat, imperfect, pastel garden roses is one of my floral passions, though I learnt the hard way that this is for some an aquired taste. I remember one occasion when I was sorely tempted to use a very boring and inoffensive bunch of pink and purple asters as a weapon. It was when a customer defiantly told me at the top of her voice that my beautiful bucketful of gorgeous garden roses were tired, old and blown. I stood my ground, and through gritted teeth tried tactfully to explain the difference between roses grown in the field and their anaemic glasshouse cousins. I calmly suggested she should take as well as her asters a gift from me of two bunches of those 'tired blown roses' for comparison. I then asked her to let me know the outcome of our little experiment, and secretly hoped never to deal with her again.

The next week she was back for more roses, and has never bought another aster since. In fact each year this customer now goes into a state of decline as the end of the rose season approaches.

These beautiful blooms came from the private garden of the wife of one of my suppliers. When she learnt of my passion for her big, blowzy, perfumed roses, she would send armfuls of them, always hidden at the back of her husband's truck, especially for me. Although they would be picked at varying stages of openness, even the most open blooms would last exceptionally well in the vase, with a perfume far stronger than that of their glasshouse-grown cousins.

The pink lupins in this
pot of flowers (left), although
pointing down, will bend
skyward within a day or two.
This is a very useful
indicator as to whether these
flowers are fresh or not.

The almost transparent petals
of pale blue iris (above) are
easily damaged. Take care to buy
iris when still closed, but
make sure you are able to see
colour, as if bought too
tight they may not open at all.

*A single tulip in a vase
will give far greater pleasure
than a hastily thrown together
mixed bunch.*

Here tulips have been teamed with narrow grey gum leaves and sheaves of ornamental black corn. The foliage was placed first into an old silverplate ice bucket with the tulips and corn then added in clumps. Some varieties of tulips may display a completely different colour inside. Always recut the stem of a tulip if it has been out of water.

Canterbury bells, peonies, roses and frilled double lisianthus are contrasted against a blue-grey pot painted with lime-wash. The matt paint weathers beautifully, making the pot a simple and inexpensive alternative to a vase. This technique can be used on cheap, uneven terracotta which, being porous, will soak up the water-based paint beautifully.

Pink cultivated tulips (left) liven up a vase containing two types of lilies and white salvia picked by the side of the road. The pollen on some of the lilies has become quite powdery and will stain whatever it comes in contact with. When the flowers are in a vase this is not so important, but when lilies are used in wedding work the stamens must be removed before they reach the powdery stage and stain the bride's dress. The beautiful clear pink of the peony (above), a lover of the cold, which, once planted, has been known to sulk for years before suddenly producing its beautiful, big, blowzy blooms. The peony has been a great favourite of painters and embroiderers in China and Japan for centuries.

Sweet peas, so easily
grown from seed, are combined
with patchwork quilt
and tiny miniature roses in this
dusky coloured posy (above).

A vase (right) of giant Russell
lupins, peonies, November lilies,
water lilies and buddleia (often
referred to as butterfly bush
because it attracts butterflies).

Water lilies can be quite
tricky: some varieties will last a
very long time whereas
others may close up at night,
making them unsuitable

for a table centrepiece for
a dinner party, although
they can be kept from closing by
placing some melted wax
in their centres.

Clumps of vine stephanotis,
tuberose and freesia (left),
all highly perfumed flowers,
are teamed with creamy
'Champagner' roses and mauve-
tipped lisianthus in a terracotta
pot which has been painted
with limewash.

Roses (above) are one of
the most rewarding flowers to
grow, with bushes often
outliving the person who planted
them. Always remove spent
blooms and this will force the
bush to continue flowering.

The same posy of flowers can be given a totally different feel by simply changing the ribbon around it and the background on which it is set. The muted posy (left) is lifted to a more cheery note by simply surrounding it with a hot pink ribbon, and altering the cool grey background to a warm pink one. This underlines the importance of background colour when flowers are placed in a room. Stock, snapdragon, pale blue iris and lisianthus make up this arrangement of pastel tones (right). Snapdragon is another of those disobedient flowers which bend in the vase. Lisianthus or prairie rose, although often expensive to buy, will reward you with weeks of delicate blooms on fine grey-green stems.

These brightly coloured miniature roses have had their stems stripped then woven through a circlet made of woody jasmine vine. Although jasmine has a beautiful perfume, its flowering period is very short. It is not a vine to be grown in a small garden as it can be very invasive if left unchecked, forming a mat of runners which make planting anything close by impossible. A good way to contain this habit if lack of space is a problem is to grow jasmine in pots. If your garden is large, however, you will forgive jasmine its invasive habit and short flowering period as the strength of its sweet heady perfume will be reward enough.

Pew decorations are very important in dressing up the venue where wedding vows will be taken, be it a church with stained glass windows, oak pews and tapestry covered cushions to kneel on, or a pretty park where council garden seats pretend to be pews and rough twine bows and ivy take the place of tulle and white satin.

If your budget is limited, don't fret, and definitely don't skimp on the flowers for the wedding party — remember, these are the flowers you and your attendants will be photographed wearing and holding. There are many ways in which you can 'rob Peter to pay Paul'.

One way is at the church. Find out if there is another wedding on the same day. If so, make contact with the other bride and you may find she is only too happy to share the cost of the flowers with you.

Should you have your own garden or access to one you can raid, do so. Even if its produce is only greenery, use this in a lavish fashion and ask your florist to provide the colour.

If you decide to take your marriage vows in a church, decorating the pews is one of the simplest ways of creating an atmosphere of celebration. I have often found that family members love to be involved, and the church flowers and pew decorations are a lovely happy way to help. It has also been my experience that many a vestry has a cupboard, in the back of which often lurks a big box of leftover pew ribbons. With the quick press of an iron and a few trails of ivy or jasmine, these renovated ribbons can simply and cheaply do the trick. Should your budget still be limited, they can be gathered up at the end of the service and used as table decorations at the reception. This can be done by the ushers while the bridal party is being photographed outside the church.

Church and pew decorations, as with bouquets, buttonhole flowers and flowers for the wedding breakfast, should all work together as a whole. For instance, a casual outdoor wedding at which masses of daisies in Mexican tin buckets are used, and garden seats double as pews, needs decoration as casual and simple as the daisies themselves. Generous bows of garden twine are far more appropriate here than cream satin ribbon.

With careful planning and forethought, you can ensure that the flowers for your wedding create a truly memorable atmosphere of celebration.

*A ball of flowers
containing gardenias, roses and
miniature daisies hangs
from the branch of a tree at an
outdoor wedding. The flowers
are cut short and used to cover a
block of damp floral foam
which has been roughly carved
into a spherical shape.*

*Believe it or not, the green fluffy
flowers in this arrangement
are actually green roses, and
have all the usual
characteristics roses are famous
for, including sharp thorns
and a strong musky scent. Here
they have been used with
roses and rosehips as well as
black tulips, seed pods and
some gold foliage, for a baroque-
style wedding held in
the autumn.*

Soft yet elegant colours of coffee
and cream (left) have
been used in an arrangement
in the apse of a church.
Blue gum makes a lovely cool foil
for the roses, peonies,
delphinium and gerberas in
pale apricot tones.
A bouquet like this one (right) is
packed with flowers, each
individually wired. Although
this bouquet is extremely
labour intensive, it is not so
difficult to put together
once one learns the basics of
wiring the flowers. Any
floral school or even your local
florist can show you how
in a few minutes. The rest is
trial and error; the
construction into a teardrop
shape takes practice.

This pretty little flower
girl wore a summer dress of red
cheesecloth with a headdress
and 'wand' of flowers to match
the bride. The wand, being
easy to carry and fun to wave
around, allowed her to be
more relaxed and fitted in with
the fairy stage she was going
through at the time, a stage
I have found most
little girls enjoy. Even the fact
that her dress was red
and not the prerequisite fairy
pink did not matter a jot
as she had the wand anyway.

The flowers for this wedding were ordered by the groom, who wanted red 'Mercedes' roses and black and gold to be the theme. Shiny red chillies, okra, baby artichokes and kangaroo paw were added. The little bridesmaids in red cheesecloth dresses also wore headdresses of chillies and kangaroo paw, and carried wands of the same flowers and vegetables.

CHAPTER

6

HINTS, TIPS AND FACTS

The question most commonly asked of a florist is, 'How long will these flowers last?', followed by the statement, 'Roses don't last!' When or how the latter misconception arose I have yet to discover. However, I suspect that many people expect too much from the queen of flowers and have rarely been fortunate enough to purchase roses which haven't been held too long in a cool room or forced or fumigated.

Choosing your flowers

Although each species of flower, and in fact each variety, will vary in its lasting power as a cut flower, the most important criterion is whether or not it is fresh when it's purchased. The most obvious way to check whether a flower is fresh or not is simply to LOOK. Not just at the flowers themselves but at their leaves and stalks, because, with the exception of some shrubs such as the glossy green camellia, many flowers will outlive their foliage. Varieties such as sunflowers and lilac are prime examples and will need their foliage stripped and replaced with other greenery before the flowers are spent. So make sure that the leaves of your lilies aren't yellow or the stems of your daisies slimy when you buy them.

A very simple way to tell if a rose is fresh is the same way you would test the ripeness of a peach or avocado: FEEL it — gently, of course. If it is soft to touch, regardless of the fact that it appears quite closed, it will probably never open. If, however, the rose is firm, it is usually fresh.

More than any other flower, each variety of rose has its own characteristics. Some, such as the beautiful white Mt Shasta, blow very quickly, yet remain big and open for almost a week. Some varieties seem to grow in the vase; some fade in colour while others darken with age. Many yellow roses will hold their colour till their last petals fall. Then there are the oldfashioned roses, many of which open to show golden stamens. Others have tight centres surrounded by loose outside petals, more closely resembling camellias than roses. Garden roses, unlike their perfect glasshouse cousins, are rarely

'peeled' by the grower and will therefore have their outside petals intact. These petals may sometimes be bruised by rain or marked by intruders such as insects or grubs, yet it is these petals which, more than anything else, give these blooms their lovely, blowzy, distinctive shape. Bearing this in mind, there are some varieties whose outside rows of petals are the ones that carry the strongest colours. For example, the very highly perfumed and aptly named 'Double Delight', whose first rows of crimson petals jump abruptly to the colour of clotted cream. With these outside petals peeled, her name would be meaningless.

The lasting power of cut flowers varies greatly between species. Many spring bulbs such as jonquils and daffodils have only a short vase life, yet, being the symbols of spring's welcome appearance, they are usually available in such abundance that I for one feel compensated for this short life.

Gerberas (above) always need stems recut before arranging. If left out of water they develop an air lock in the stem, inhibiting moisture from being drawn up to the head.

It is often unnecessary to untie bunches when arranging flowers (right). Leave the growers twine in place not only to keeep the bunch together but as a decorative tool.

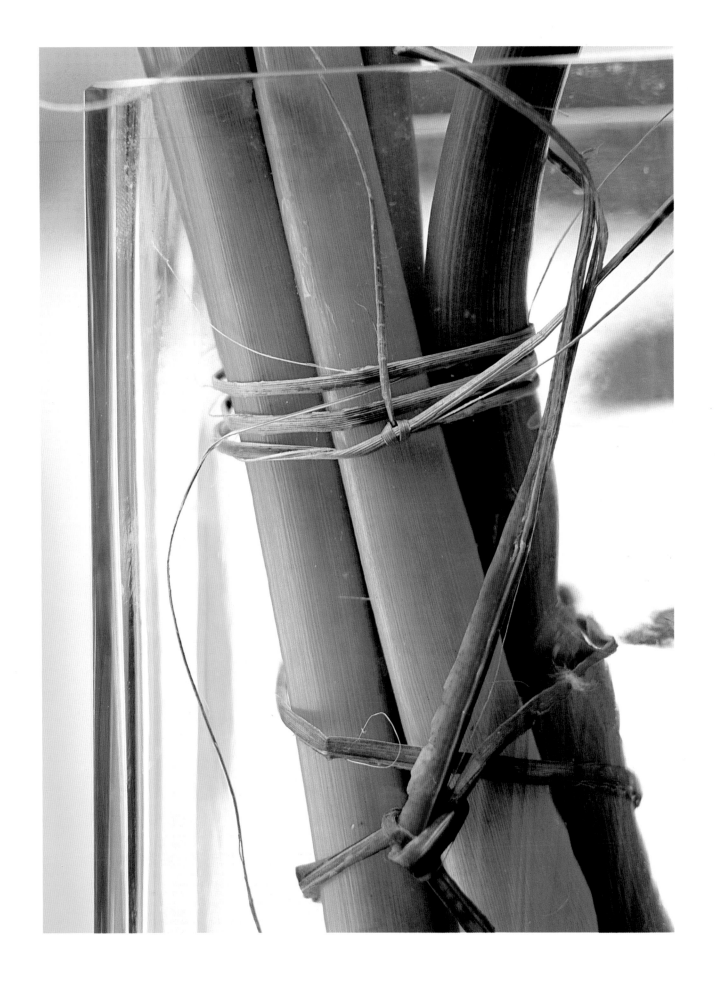

*An old tiled horse trough
in the courtyard of an historic
house is filled with a
profusion of clumps of flowers.
Using this same system of
clumping colours and varieties
together when arranging
flowers in a vase will make a
successfully bold statement.*

Long-lasting varieties such as chrysanthemums, alstromeria
and lilies can go on for weeks, and hardy varieties such as
South Africa's proteas and many Australian native flowers last
so long they may well need dusting.

So, unless you have purchased your flowers for a special
event such as a dinner party or celebration, where you will
need them to be at their peak and open, try to choose flowers
that are either in bud or have buds still to open. One notable
exception to this rule is the iris. This flower is often picked
too tight to allow it either the time or the strength to unfurl
before it fades.

Care of cut flowers

In order to maximise the life of cut flowers, there are several very simple rules to follow. Now that you have purchased your flowers and ascertained that they are fresh, the most important and most frequently overlooked rule is that all flowers must have their stems recut before being placed in water.

The reason for this is quite simple. When a flower is cut and the stem exposed to the air for a period of 15 minutes or more, air bubbles will form in the first 20 to 30 mm (inch or so) of the stem, thus causing a blockage. The simplest method to remedy this situation is to recut the stems, preferably under water.

This method works particularly well for varieties such as roses, chrysanthemums, snapdragons and gerberas.

Apart from the curly question of how long flowers will last, I am often asked what, if anything, should be added to the water to prolong the life of cut flowers. This is often followed by a string of remedies, old wives' tales and general folklore ranging from the addition of headache tablets to putting a penny in the vase.

Now for the facts. Once flowers are harvested, they are immediately separated from their food source. If you were starving, you would find little nourishment from aspirin. Once this is understood, it becomes obvious that a solution which contains food for the severed flowers will enable the buds to open and the flowers to keep growing.

Floral preserver

There are several excellent commercially available floral preservers to choose from, and most enlightened florists will stock them. However, it is a simple task to make up a solution of floral preserver at home using three of the most basic ingredients normally found on the shelves of even the most depleted pantries such as mine. These ingredients are: sugar, bleach and vinegar.

Allium giganteum, irises, artichokes and honeycomb ginger are held in place in a giant fishbowl with the aid of lemons. This little trick is especially useful if you have a vase which is too large or too deep for your flowers. As the lemons are quite heavy, however, it is best to do the arrangement in situ.

PIANO • VOCAL • GUITAR

80's COUNTRY GOLD

ISBN 0-88188-426-X

HAL LEONARD PUBLISHING CORPORATION

Home Office:
960 East Mark Street
Winona MN 55987

National Sales Office:
8112 West Bluemound Road
Milwaukee WI 53213

ANY DAY NOW

Words and Music by BOB HILLIARD
and BURT F. BACHARACH

AS LONG AS I'M ROCKIN' WITH YOU

Words and Music by KIERAN KANE
and BRUCE CHANNEL

6

Additional Verses:

3. Wherever I'm workin', whatever it's payin'
   It doesn't matter long as it's workin' with you
   Workin' with you.

4. These things I believe in some people call dreamin'
   It doesn't matter long as I'm dreamin' with you
   Dreamin' with you.
   (CHORUS)

BABY I LIED

Words and Music by RAFE VANHOY,
RORY BOURKE and DEBORAH ALLEN

BABY'S GOT HER BLUE JEANS ON

Words and Music by BOB McDILL

Down on the cor-ner by the traf-fic light ev'-ry-bod-y's look-in'

as she goes by.___ They turn their heads___ and they watch her till___ she's gone.___

Lord, have mer-cy! Ba - by's got her blue jeans on.___

CAN'T KEEP A GOOD MAN DOWN

Words and Music by
BOB CORBIN

I thought it was for-ev-er, I thought it would last.

Got-ta try to make it a page of my past. You did-n't e-ven say good-bye

when you slammed that door. Now I'm

THE CHAIR

Medium Slow

Words and Music by HANK COCHRAN
and DEAN DILLON

COULD I HAVE THIS DANCE

Words and Music by WAYLAND HOLYFIELD
and BOB HOUSE

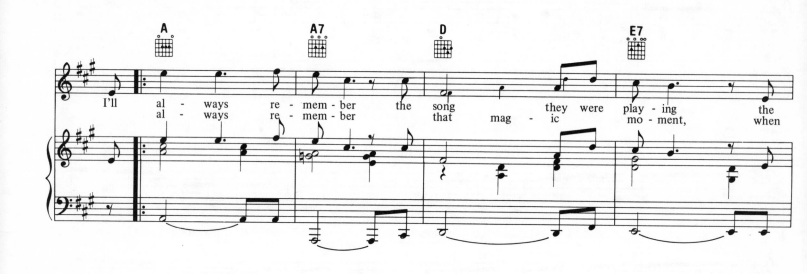

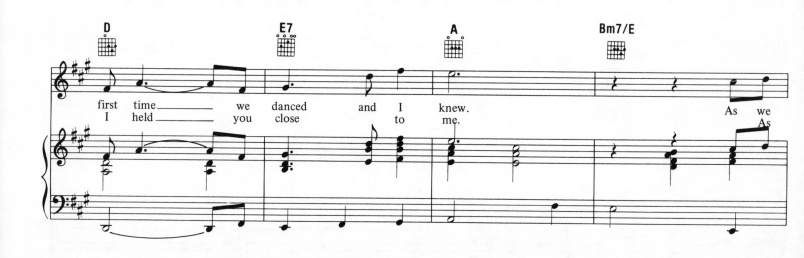

DON'T CHEAT IN OUR HOME TOWN

Words and Music by RAY PENNINGTON
and ROY MARCUM

Additional lyrics

Now, there are no secrets in this little country town,
Everyone knows everyone for miles and miles around.
Your bright eyes and your sweet smile are driving me insane.
You think it's smart to break my heart and run down my name.

To Chorus

CRYING MY HEART OUT OVER YOU

Words and Music by CARL BUTLER,
MARIJOHN WILKIN, LOUISE CERTAIN and GLADYS STACEY

GOD BLESS THE U.S.A.

Words and Music by
LEE GREENWOOD

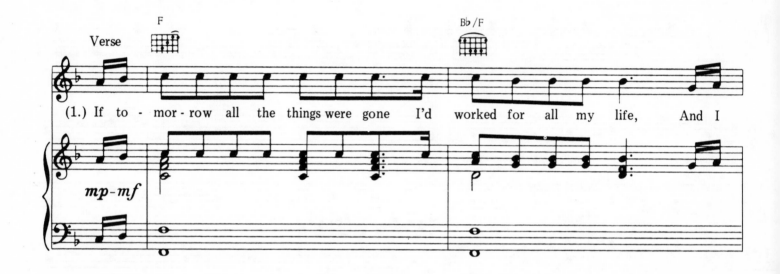

MCA MUSIC

HANG ON TO YOUR HEART

Words and Music by SONNY LEMAIRE
and J.P. PENNINGTON

HE STOPPED LOVING HER TODAY

Words and Music by
BOBBY BRADDOCK & CURLY PUTMAN

Verse 3:

He kept some letters by his bed, dated 1962.
He had underlined in red every single, "I love you".

Verse 4:

I went to see him just today, oh, but I didn't see no tears;
All dressed up to go away, first time I'd seen him smile in years.
(To Chorus:)

Verse 5: *(Spoken)*

You know, she came to see him one last time.
We all wondered if she would.
And it came running through my mind,
This time he's over her for good. (To Chorus:)

HONEY
(Open That Door)

Words and Music by MEL TILLIS

Honey, _____ Honey, _____

Hon-ey won't you o-pen that door?__ This is your sweet dad-dy don't you love me no more?__ It's

cold out-side, let me sleep on the floor,__ Hon-ey won't you o-pen that door?_____

I DON'T WANT TO BE A MEMORY

Words and Music by SONNY LEMAIRE
and J.P. PENNINGTON

So lay back down_ and let's talk _____ it o - ver,_

I don't want to be a mem - 'ry.

To Coda

Don't you re - mem - ber how it used to be When we were so in love._

We spent the nights in a two room flat Drink-ing wine from a cof - fee cup._

I know you've had oth-er lov-ers,___ that's all his-to-ry___

___ I've got to know that you'll let me be the last __ one To share your com-pan-y.___

I don't want to be a mem-o-ry___

I LOVED 'EM EVERY ONE

Words and Music by
PHIL SAMPSON

Moderately bright

I WAS COUNTRY
WHEN COUNTRY WASN'T COOL

Words and Music by KYE FLEMING
and DENNIS MORGAN

Verse 2:
I remember circling the drive-in,
Pulling up, and turning down George Jones.
I remember when no one was looking,
I was putting peanuts in my coke.
I took a lot of kidding, 'cause I never did fit in;
Now look at everybody trying to be what I was then;
I was country, when country wasn't cool.

Verse 3:
They called us country bumpkins for sticking to our roots;
I'm just glad we're in a country where we're all free to choose;
I was country, when country wasn't cool.

I WOULDN'T HAVE MISSED IT FOR THE WORLD

Words and Music by KYE FLEMING,
DENNIS MORGAN and CHARLES QUILLEN

1. Our paths may nev-er cross___ a-gain;
2. (see additional lyrics)

may-be my heart___ will nev-er mend,___

but I'm glad for all the good___ times.

You brought me so___

Verse 2.
They say that all good things must end.
Love comes and goes just like the wind.
You've got your dreams to follow,
But if I had the chance tomorrow,
You know I'd do it all again.
(To Chorus)

ISLANDS IN THE STREAM

Moderately Slow Rock

Words and Music by BARRY GIBB,
MAURICE GIBB and ROBIN GIBB

Ba - by when I met you there was peace un - known.
I can't live with - out you if the love was gone.

I set out to get you with a fine tooth comb. I was soft in - side__ there__
ev - 'ry - thing is noth - ing if you got no - one and you__ did walk in the night__ slow-

__ was some - thing go - in on.__
- ly lo - sin sight of the real thing.__ But

I'LL NEVER STOP LOVING YOU

Words and Music by DAVE LOGGINS
and J.D. MARTIN

Medium Slow

I just might take to leav-in' in the mid-dle of the night, and

I might not be here in the morn-ing light. But I'll nev-er stop lov-in' you,

lov-in' you. I might be

MCA MUSIC

LET'S FALL TO PIECES TOGETHER

Words and Music by TOMMY ROCCO,
DICKEY LEE and JOHNNY RUSSELL

A LITTLE GOOD NEWS

Words and Music by CHARLIE BLACK,
RORY BOURKE and TOMMY ROCCO

Slow 4

I rolled out this morn-ing the kids had the morn-ing news show on; Bry-ant Gum-bel was talk-in' 'bout the fight-ing in Leb-a-non; Some sen-a-tor was squawk-ing 'bout the bad e-con-o-my. It's gon-na get worse you see, we need a change in pol-i-cy.

MAKIN' UP FOR LOST TIME

Words and Music by DAVE LOGGINS
and GARY MORRIS

MCA MUSIC

MORNING DESIRE

Words and Music by
DAVE LOGGINS

Here it is sev-en in the A. M.,__ its gon-na take more than wak-in'__ to rise__ me.__

MCA MUSIC

OLDER WOMEN

Words and Music by JAMIE O'HARA

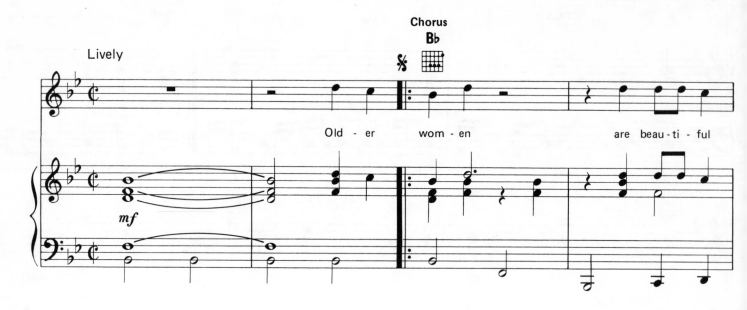

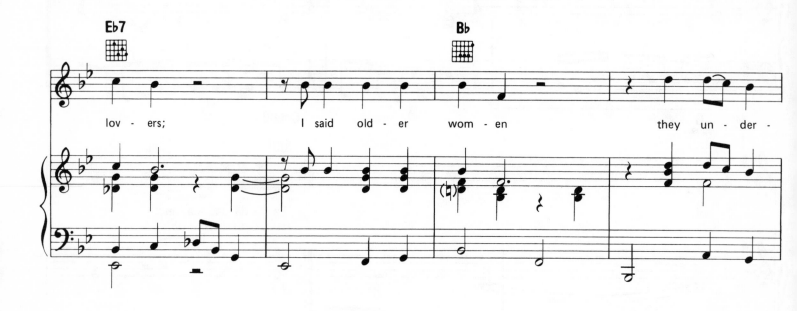

STAND BY ME

Words and Music by BEN E. KING,
MIKE STOLLER and JERRY LEIBER

SMOKY MOUNTAIN RAIN

Words and Music by KYE FLEMING
and DENNIS MORGAN

I thumbed my way from L. A. back to Knox - ville;
I waved a dies - el down out - side a ca - fe;

I found out those bright lights ain't where I be - long.
He said that he was going as far as Gat - lin - burg.

From a phone booth, in the rain, I called to
I climbed up in the cab, All wet and cold and

SOMEBODY SHOULD LEAVE

Words and Music by HARLAN HOWARD
and CHICK RAINS

You need the kids,___ and they___ need me.

Some-bod-y should leave,___ but we hate to_____ give in.

We keep hop-in' some-how___ we might need each oth-er a-gain.___

SWINGIN'

Words and Music by JOHN DAVID ANDERSON
and LIONEL A. DELMORE

With a strong beat

1. There's _____ a lit-tle girl in our neigh-bor-hood. Her
2.3. (See additional lyrics)

name is Char-lotte John-son, and she's real-ly look-ing good. I had to go and see her, so I

called her on the phone. I walked o-ver to her house, _____ and this was go-in' on: 2. Her

Verse 2.
Her brother was on the sofa
Eatin' chocolate pie.
Her mama was in the kitchen
Cuttin' chicken up to fry.
Her daddy was in the backyard
Rollin' up a garden hose.
I was on the porch with Charlotte
Feelin' love down to my toes,
And we was swingin'. *(To Chorus:)*

Verse 3.
Now Charlotte, she's a darlin';
She's the apple of my eye.
When I'm on the swing with her
It makes me almost high.
And Charlotte is my lover.
And she has been since the spring.
I just can't believe it started
On her front porch in the swing. *(To Chorus:)*

WHAT'S FOREVER FOR

Words and Music by RAFE VANHOY

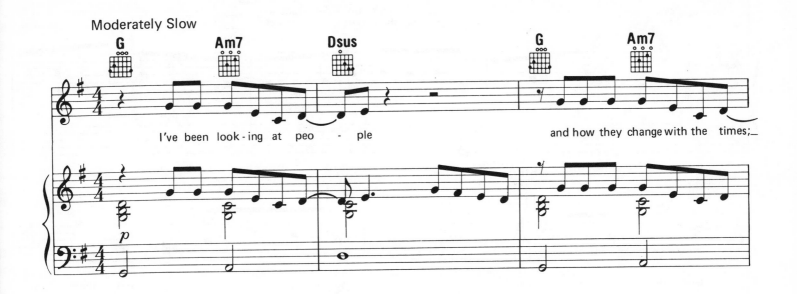

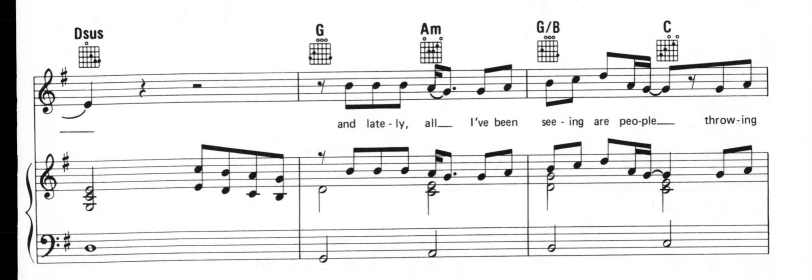

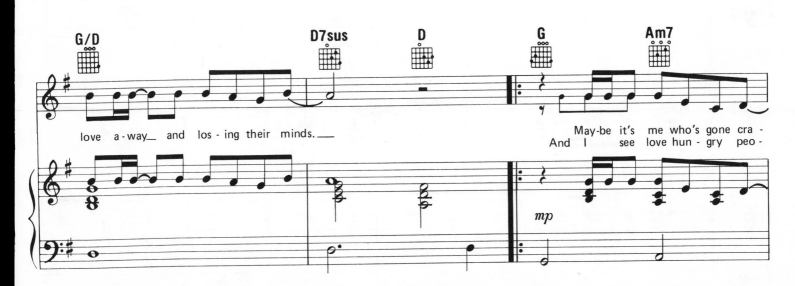

WHY NOT ME

Medium Country

Words and Music by HARLAN HOWARD,
SONNY THROCKMORTON and BRENT MAHER